Little
Piping Plover

WRITTEN & ILLUSTRATED BY

J. ROACH-EVANS

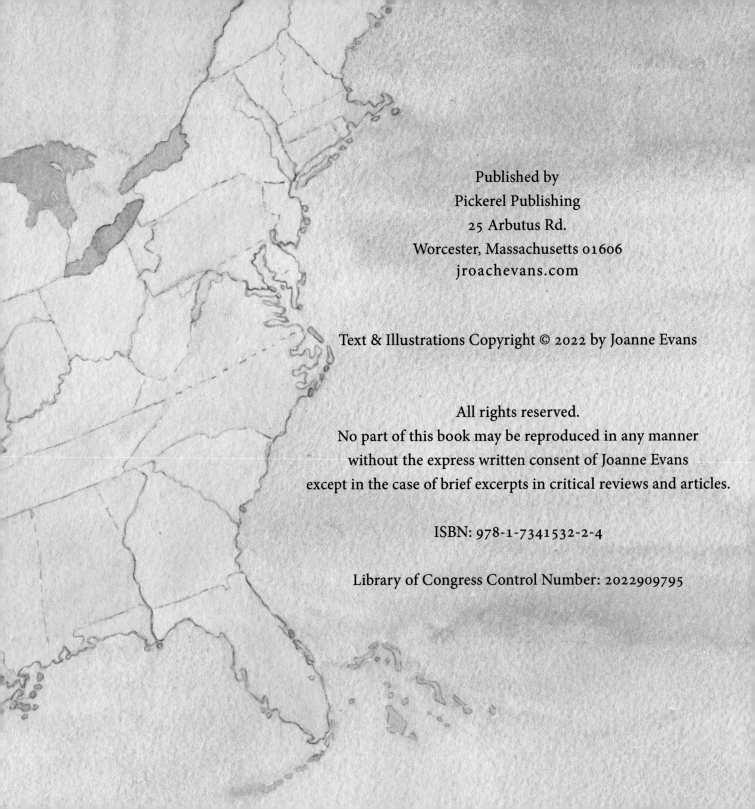

Published by
Pickerel Publishing
25 Arbutus Rd.
Worcester, Massachusetts 01606
jroachevans.com

ISBN: 978-1-7341532-2-4

Library of Congress Control Number: 2022909795

Dedicated to

my mother, Marianne

with love

♡

It is springtime at the seashore.

Two tiny shorebirds called piping plovers

take turns sitting on their nest in the sand.

They are keeping their eggs safe and warm.

Special people put up fences to protect the plovers while they are nesting. This beach has a yellow rope that lets the beachgoers know to stay away from the nesting area.

The weeks go by and the plover parents watch over the eggs.

As the days get warmer,

lots of people come to the beach to play and rest.

The plover parents need to keep themselves and their eggs safe

on such a busy beach.

People help watch over the plovers during the busiest times of the summer when the eggs and chicks are most vulnerable.

They do their best to tend
their eggs each day and
night for weeks.

Then one day....

Piping plovers typically lay three to four eggs. Seashells and stones help to hide the eggs from foxes, racoons, rats, seagulls, and other creatures that would eat plover eggs.

...an egg cracks and slowly opens and a little chick tumbles out.

Not long after, another egg cracks and another chick breaks

out of the shell.

After they hatch, the little birds take a moment to rest.

Breaking out of a shell is hard work!

The last egg to hatch reveals the littlest plover.

She is the color of dry sand

and looks as soft

as a cloud in the sky.

She blends in well with the beach sand,

stones, and seashells.

This is called camouflage.

The littlest plover joins her siblings

on their big feet as they look for bugs to eat.

The plovers can run around, but they cannot yet fly.

Their flight feathers will need time to grow.

Until they can fly,

their camouflage helps protect them.

If they sense danger, they will lay low and stay still,

hiding under their parents' wings or in the beach grass.

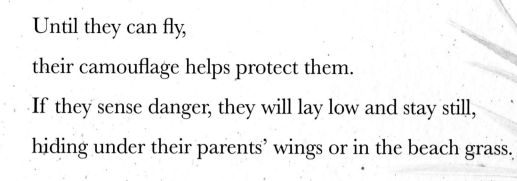

Camouflage is when an animal's coloring blends in well with their habitat. Lots of animals use camouflage to hide. A habitat is the environment where they live.

Can you find the littlest plover?

Can you find her mom hiding too?

Little plover and her siblings can't hide forever though -

they will need to get down to the water's edge to eat.

But my, what a busy beach!

They may have to run around coolers,

umbrellas, blankets, and chairs!

Little plover might even need

to dodge

a big beach ball!

Watch out little plover!

Little plover and her siblings are hungry and they must eat.

They run down to the shoreline to search for food

in the seaweed and wet sand.

It's not easy, but it's worth it to find a tasty treat.

They need to eat well and grow strong.

Piping plovers eat marine worms, bugs, little crabs, and beach hoppers.

They need to be strong enough to fly.

Every day little plover and her family

go down to the shoreline and search for food.

*Piping plovers will usually try to avoid humans,
but there is not a lot of space on a busy beach.*

Every day their wings grow stronger
and bigger too.

Over a month goes by and little plover's wings change from soft down to strong flight feathers that can catch the wind. Soon she can fly to the water's edge and back again - Zoom!

This is much safer than running the whole way.

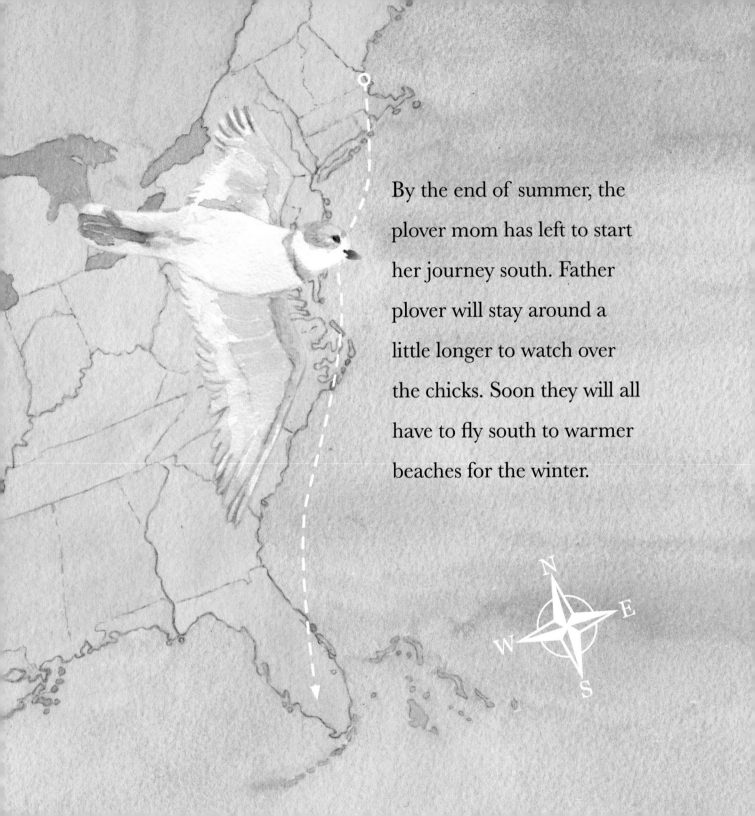

By the end of summer, the plover mom has left to start her journey south. Father plover will stay around a little longer to watch over the chicks. Soon they will all have to fly south to warmer beaches for the winter.

Will little plover know when to go?

Is she ready to fly off on her own?

She will know when it is time to fly south.

She will sense it in the wind
and she will take flight.

Little plover has learned a lot over the summer.

Our little plover is already a survivor.

She has grown up on a very busy beach.

ABOUT PIPING PLOVERS

Piping plovers live and breed on the Northern Great Plains, Great Lakes, and the Atlantic Coast. Piping plovers almost disappeared from New England beaches because they need safe, undisturbed places to nest, but through the efforts of many people their numbers have been slowly climbing.

Since 1986 many people have been helping plovers to survive by fencing off their nesting grounds, and putting protective wiring over their nests to protect them from seagulls, crows, foxes, coyotes, skunks, raccoons, rats, cats, and dogs. Volunteers also help by educating the public and watching over the flightless chicks as they navigate the busy beaches. Piping plover eggs and chicks are so small and blend in so well with the sand that people can easily disturb or damage them without even realizing it. You can do your part by being aware of the piping plover families and giving them lots of space.

NOTE: Since 1997 the number of nesting pairs of piping plovers on Seabrook Beach and Hampton Beach has ranged from 5 to 13, resulting in 4 to 47 chicks.
Source: www.wildlife.state.nh.us/nongame/ project-plover.html

Greetings from
Hampton Beach, N. H.

AREA CLOSED

This area is important breeding territory for

Piping Plovers –
a federally threatened
state endangered species.

Your help is needed
to avoid disturbance to
piping plovers, their nests and chicks.

PLEASE DO NOT ENTER

WHAT YOU CAN DO
TO HELP PIPING PLOVERS

- **Give them lots of space.**
*If you see a bird pretending to have a broken wing...
you are too close!*

- **DO NOT CHASE THEM or go near their nests.**

- **Do not fly kites near plover nesting areas.**
They think kites are predatory birds.

- **Keep all pets leashed and away from the
plover nests.**

- **Fill in deep holes and moats in the sand.**
Baby plovers fall in and can't get out!

- **Do not feed seagulls or leave food
on the beach.** *Food attracts predators
that will also eat plovers or their eggs.*

Beach hopper

ACKNOWLEDGEMENTS

Special thanks to my dear friend, Sherri Gionet, for helping me to see this story with new eyes. A big thank you to Dorie Stolley of the Goldenrod Foundation and Lisa Hutchings from Joppa Flats Mass Audubon for their helpful comments and suggestions. I'd also like to thank my readers, including my extended family, my teacher/neighbors Patricia O'Connell and Kerry Trotto, and Gisa Nico of Butterfly Preschool, for their time and thoughtful edits and suggestions.

To my amazing editor Erin Oliveira for the hard work she has done on this book and others - I could not have published these books without your wisdom and expertise as a marine biologist and scientific editor.

A big shout out and thank you to Shawn Carey of Migration Productions for the generous use of his video and photographic images as reference for several of my watercolors. I am also indebted to Jim Fenton for graciously letting me use his photo of chicks in the nest for my model of little plover. I am most grateful to everyone for their help and support!

RESOURCES:

Maine Audubon
Mass Audubon
MassWildlife
New Hampshire Fish & Game
The Cornell Lab of Ornithology
The Goldenrod Foundation
U.S. Fish and Wildlife Service

To see more about piping plovers check out
these great websites and YouTube channel:

Jim Fenton photography
https://www.natureandwings.com/Wildlife/
Migration Productions Exploring the Natural World
https://www.youtube.com/channel
Migration Productions Exploring the Natural World.com

Joanne Roach-Evans is the author and illustrator of several
seashore books: Seashells, Treasures from the Northeast Coast;
Seaweed, Marine Algae from the Northeast Coast;
Marine Animals from the Northeast Coast;
and Marine Birds from the Northeast Coast.
If you've enjoyed this book please leave a review on Amazon!
You can also check out Joanne's YouTube videos @ jroachevans.com

AFTERWORD

One summer in late August I saw a lone piping plover youngster on Hampton Beach in New Hampshire. I had previously photographed adults in Maine and on Cape Cod in Massachusetts, but this particular plover's presence struck me as nothing short of amazing considering the popularity of Hampton Beach. I was so inspired by this little bird's survival that I just had to write this book.

Piping plovers face difficult challenges at many beaches on the East Coast and

elsewhere. Hatching out of their eggs right in to an environment as busy as Hampton Beach is especially challenging for the plovers.

I'd like to thank all those that have endeavored to save these birds and spent countless hours working on their behalf. I'm so grateful to New Hampshire Fish and Game and the volunteers for protecting the plovers at Hampton Beach. Without their efforts, I would have never witnessed this little miracle of survival.

Made in the USA
Middletown, DE
25 August 2022

71972822R00020